Icebreakers

Written by Jo Windsor

PIERRE RADISSON

T0362781

CONTENTS

Why We Have Icebreakers

In some places it is so cold in winter that the water freezes. The ice is very thick. No ships can come and go through the ice. When this happens, a ship called an icebreaker is used to break up the ice.

Icebreakers are very big ships made for breaking ice. Icebreakers help keep the seas cleared of ice so other ships can move from place to place. They make sure that ships can go through the frozen water all winter long.

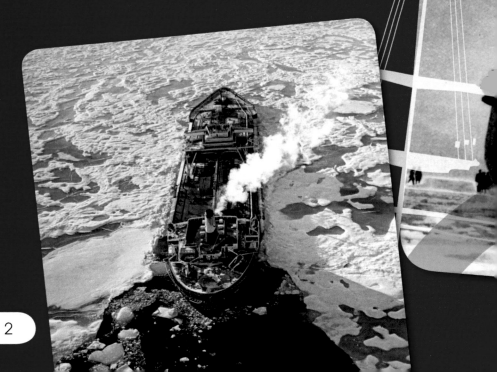

an icebreaker in 1911

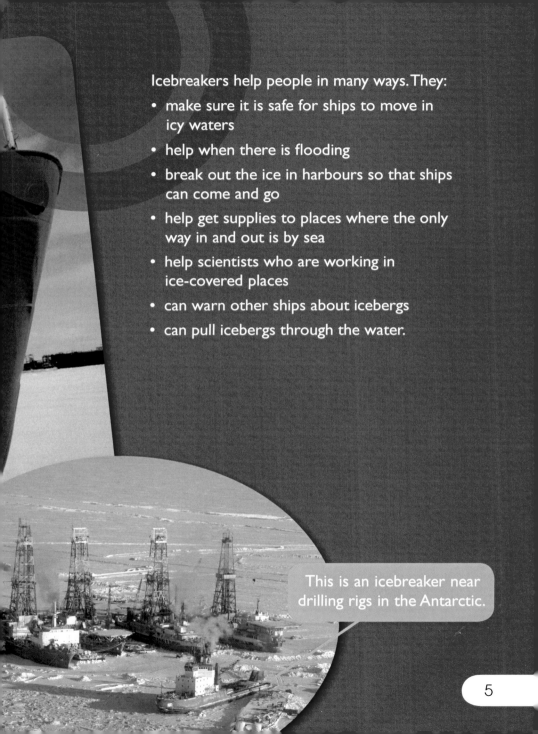

Icebreakers help people in many ways. They:

- make sure it is safe for ships to move in icy waters
- help when there is flooding
- break out the ice in harbours so that ships can come and go
- help get supplies to places where the only way in and out is by sea
- help scientists who are working in ice-covered places
- can warn other ships about icebergs
- can pull icebergs through the water.

This is an icebreaker near drilling rigs in the Antarctic.

What Icebreakers Look Like

Icebreakers are built in a special shape.
They are much wider than other ships.
Some icebreakers can be 30 metres wide.
This helps the icebreaker make a path through
the ice that is wide enough for other ships to
go through.

Icebreakers are very heavy ships. The ship builders have to make them very strong. The hull, or frame, of the ship is made of steel that is very thick. This stops the ship from cracking when it moves quickly through the ice.

hull

bow

The front of the ship is called the bow. The hull under the bow is shaped like a knife. This helps the icebreaker cut through the ice.

The back of the ship is called the stern. Huge propellers are under the stern. Icebreakers have powerful engines that turn these huge propellers. They push the ship forward through the ice. Sometimes the ice can be more than two metres thick.

propellers

What Icebreakers Do

1. The icebreaker moves forward. The bow of the icebreaker slides up on the ice. This puts a lot of weight on the ice.

2. The icebreaker keeps moving forward and up onto the ice.

3. The weight of the icebreaker breaks up the ice in big pieces.

4. The icebreaker moves forward through the water and the broken ice is pushed out of the way.

This happens again and again, as the icebreaker clears a way through the ice.

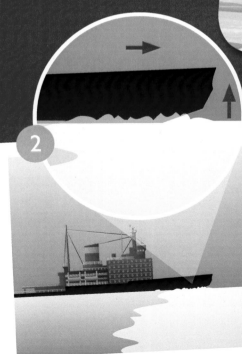

The Crew of an Icebreaker

captain

The crew in the control room control everything on the ship.

There may be more than 100 people in the crew on an icebreaker. The captain controls the icebreaker from the top of the ship. The crew are trained to work in very difficult and dangerous places.

Engineers look after the engines.

Navigators decide which way the ship will go.

Radio operators talk to people on other ships.

The crew need to be ready to take an icebreaker where other ships cannot go.

Ice and icebergs are a problem for ships, but not for icebreakers. They can easily break up ice with their strong hulls.

Icebreakers and their crews help other ships keep sailing. They make a way in and out of places that would be cut off by the ice.

Index

Icebreakers is a Report.

A report has a topic:

> ## Icebreakers

A report has headings:

> ### Why We Have Icebreakers

> ### What Icebreakers Look Like

> ### What Icebreakers Do

> ### The Crew of an Icebreaker

Some information is put under headings.

Why We Have Icebreakers

- to clear icy seas
- to clear harbours

Information can be shown in other ways.

This report has ...

Labels   Captions   Flow Diagram

Bullet Points   Photographs

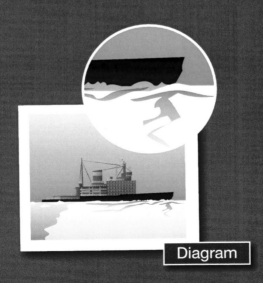

Diagram

Guide Notes

Title: Icebreakers

Stage: Fluency

Text Form: Informational Report

Approach: Guided Reading

Processes: Thinking Critically, Exploring Language, Processing Information

Written and Visual Focus: Contents Page, Captions, Labels, Bullet Points, Flow Diagram, Index

THINKING CRITICALLY
(sample questions)

Before Reading – Establishing Prior Knowledge
* What do you know about ships that can break through ice?

Visualising the Text Content
* What might you expect to see in this book?
* What form of writing do you think will be used by the author?

Look at the contents page and index. Encourage the students to think about the information and make predictions about the text content.

After Reading – Interpreting the Text
* Why do you think it is important for ships to be able to move through the water all year round?
* Why do you think an icebreaker would have to pull an iceberg through the water?
* Do you think an icebreaker is a powerful ship? Why do you think that?
* Do you think an icebreaker could cut through ice that was thicker than two metres? Why do you think that?
* What do you think might happen if an icebreaker's engines stopped?
* Why do you think there are so many crew members aboard an icebreaker?
* What do you know about icebreakers that you didn't know before?
* What in the book helped you understand the information?
* What questions do you have after reading the text?

EXPLORING LANGUAGE

Terminology
Photograph credits, index, contents page, imprint information, ISBN number